This book belongs to :

....

....

I spy with my little eye something beginning with ...

A is for Angel

I spy with my little eye something beginning with ...

B is for Bell

I spy with my little eye something beginning with ...

C is for Candle

I spy with my little eye something beginning with ...

D is for Decoration

I spy with my little eye something beginning with ...

E is for

Snowman

I spy with my little eye something beginning with ...

I spy with my little eye something beginning with ...

G is for Gift

I spy with my little eye something beginning with ...

H is for

HAT

I spy with my little eye something beginning with ...

I is for Imp

I spy with my little eye something beginning with ...

I spy with my little eye something beginning with ...

K is for King

I spy with my little eye something beginning with ... L

L is for

Lights

I spy with my little eye something beginning with ...

I spy with my little eye something beginning with ...

n is for

Nuts

I spy with my little eye something beginning with ...

 is for

Ornament

I spy with my little eye something beginning with ...

P is for Pudding

I spy with my little eye something beginning with ...

Q is for

Quince

I spy with my little eye something beginning with ...

R is for Reindeer

I spy with my little eye something beginning with ...

S is for Stocking

I spy with my little eye something beginning with ...

T is for Turkey

I spy with my little eye something beginning with ...

U is for

Unicorn

I spy with my little eye something beginning with ...

V is for Vanilla

I spy with my little eye something beginning with ...

W is for

Wreath

I spy with my little eye something beginning with ...

X is for X-MAS LIGHTS

I spy with my little eye something beginning with ...

Y is for

Yule log

I spy with my little eye something beginning with ...

Z is for Zucchini

Printed in the USA
CPSIA information can be obtained
at www.ICGtesting.com
LVHW061124301124
798008LV00048B/3022